Math Counts

Sorting

Introduction

In keeping with the major goals of the National Council of Teachers of Mathematics Curriculum and Evaluation Standards, children will become mathematical problem solvers, learn to communicate mathematically, and learn to reason mathematically by using the series Math Counts.

Pattern, Shape, and Size may be investigated first—in any sequence.

Sorting, Counting, and Numbers may be used next, followed by Time, Length, Weight, and Capacity.

Ramona G. Choos, Professor of Mathematics, Senior Adviser to the Dean of Continuing Education, Chicago State University; Sponsor for Chicago Elementary Teachers' Mathematics Club

About this Book

Mathematics is a part of a child's world. It is not only interpreting numbers or mastering tricks of addition or multiplication. Mathematics is about ideas. These ideas have been developed to explain particular qualities such as size, weight, and height, as well as relationships and comparisons. Yet all too often the important part that an understanding of mathematics will play in a child's development is forgotten or ignored.

Most adults can solve simple mathematical tasks without the need for counters, beads, or fingers. Young children find such abstractions almost impossible to master. They need to see, talk, touch, and experiment.

The photographs and text in these books have been chosen to encourage talk about topics that are essentially mathematical. By talking, the young reader can explore some of the central concepts that support mathematics. It is on an understanding of these concepts that a child's future mastery of mathematics will be built.

Henry Pluckrose

1995 Childrens Press® Edition
© 1994 Watts Books, London, New York, Sydney
All rights reserved.
Printed in China.
Published simultaneously in Canada.
33 34 35 R 19 18 17 16

Sorting

By Henry Pluckrose

Mathematics Consultant: Ramona G. Choos,
Professor of Mathematics

CHILDRENS PRESS ®
CHICAGO

What a mix-up.
How could you sort it out?

Here are some animals,

5

some buttons,

four cars,

and six pencils.

8

Look how the animals have been sorted.
Why have they been grouped like this?

The pencils have been sorted in a special way too.

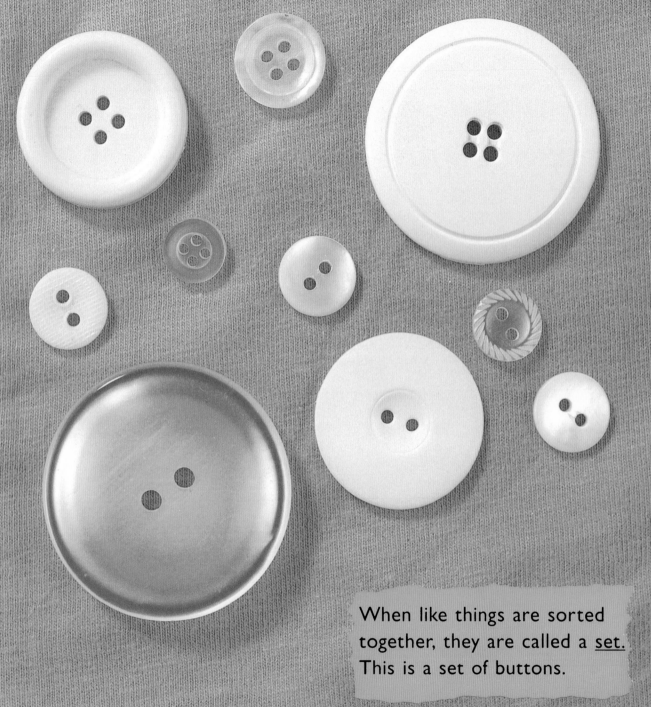

When like things are sorted together, they are called a <u>set.</u> This is a set of buttons.

11

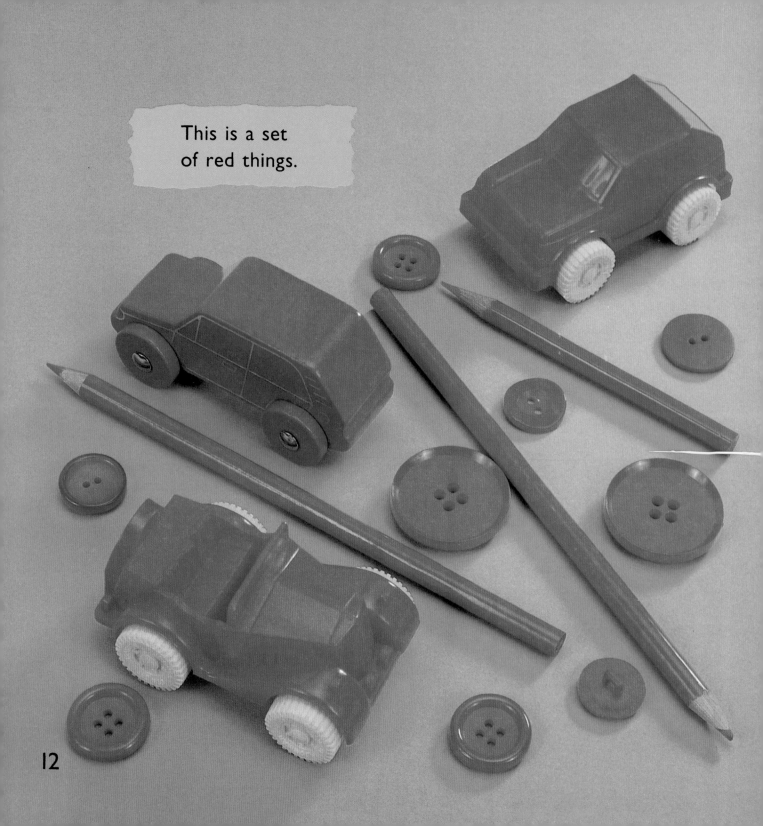

This is a set
of red things.

What kind of set
is this?

How many different ways
could you sort these flowers

and these fruits?

Things that make up a set
have something in common.
These are all toys

and these things are all found in a bathroom.

What do these things
have in common

18

and these?

We talk about
sets of
trains,

20

a set of books,

and even sets of bingo cards.

This is a set of dishes.

This is a container for silverware.
The spaces are used
to "set" the knives, forks, and spoons.

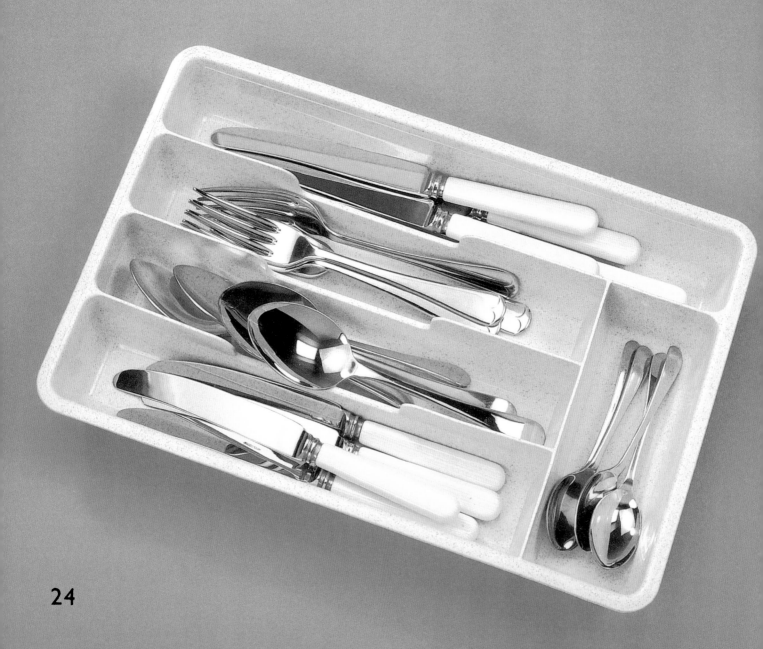

When you set a table, each person has a place. What do you notice about each setting?

25

Sometimes all the things in a set
are identical.
Each wheel on a car
has to be exactly the same.
Would the extra wheel fit this car?

26

There is something special about this set of dolls. How do they fit together?

If you go into a supermarket
you will find vegetables.
They are grouped together.

SARDE
£ 4.000

TRIGLIE SCOGLIO
£ 24.000 kg

CANESTRELLI
£ 9.500 kg

SEPPIE PULITE
£ 11.000 kg

GAMBERI IMPERIALI
£ 39.000 kg

Are the same kinds of fish
grouped together?

What about the bread?
How does this help you find
the things you want to buy?

Collect a group of objects.
See how many different ways
you can sort them.

Library of Congress Cataloging-in-Publication Data

Pluckrose, Henry Arthur.
    sorting / Henry Pluckrose.
        p. cm.
    Originally published: London; New York: F. Watts, 1988.
    (Math counts)
    Includes index.
    ISBN 0-516-45458-7
    I. Set theory — Juvenile literature. [I. Set theory.] I. Title.
    QA248.P58 1995
    511.3'2 — dc20
                                                        94-38004
                                                           CIP
                                                           AC

Photographic credit: Chris Fairclough, 4, 5, 6, 7, 8, 9, 10, 11, 12, 13, 14, 15, 16, 17, 18, 19, 21, 23, 24, 25, 26, 27, 29, 30, 31; Unicorn Stock Photos, © Joel Dexter, 20, © Ed Birch, 22; ZEFA, 28
Editor: Ruth Thomson
Design: Chloë Cheesman

INDEX